Oceaness:

Blue Ecology Edition

By
Michael D. Blackstock

Also by
Michael D. Blackstock

Faces in the Forest:
First Nations art created on living trees
(McGill-Queen's University Press, 2001)

Salmon Run:
A florilegium of aboriginal ecological poetry
(Wyget Books, 2005)

How to Make a Good Decision:
A five step guide to making everyday decisions
(Wyget Books, 2015)

Library and Archives Canada Cataloguing in Publication

Blackstock, Michael D., 1961-
Oceaness / by Michael D. Blackstock.

Poems.
ISBN 978-0-9736765-2-5

1.   Indians of North America—Poetry.
2.   Ecology – Poetry. 3. Water — Poetry. I. Title.

PS8603.L28O34 2010 C811'.6 C2010-906546-8

Instagram: blueecology.mb
Twitter: @blueecology

The book is set in Calibri, Aharoni and American Typewriter. Art work and
photographs are by Michael D. Blackstock. A print on demand and
ecologically responsible book. The production of this book did not rely on
public funding.[1]

---

[1]During the Second World War, Winston Churchill's finance minister said Britain
should cut arts funding to support the war effort. Churchill's response: "Then what
are we fighting for?"

Thank you to the Indigenous Elders who taught me about the spirit of water

Thank you to all that support Blue Ecology

People like to share books. It's environmental. Share this one, and log in your name, date & place to track the journey of this book.

Name	Date	Place

Weather is water's mood

Go to the water, to read this book

Oceaness: An ocean-meadow of magical snow crystals, at Lac Le Jeune,
British Columbia (Blackstock, 2008)

Contents

Blue Ecology & Climate Change

Over the past 18 years, I have conducted independent research with my Elders about water. Gitxsan Chief Mary Mackenzie, shared during the Delgamuukw court case, her knowledge of how the *halayt* (shaman or healer) gained power and learned their songs from the waterfall:

> *Now, to get that—those songs, these people [halayts], they're taken out where there's a waterfall and they stay there for sometime. And this person would go to this waterfall and sit by this waterfall by the hours and then you hear the echo of the waterfall and they listen to that and they say little by little there's words coming out from that waterfall and this they have to—they have to remember.*

Blue ecology is an ecological philosophy, which emerged from my interweaving of Indigenous and Western thought to acknowledge water's (i.e. fresh and salt) essential rhythmical life-spirit and central functional role in generating, sustaining, receiving and ultimately unifying life on Earth Mother. No dichotomy between the living and elemental exists in Blue Ecology: Earth Mother is an inter-connected whole. The vision of Blue Ecology is to: embrace a water-first approach to planning human interventions in the environment. Blue Ecology is about creating hope in the face of climate change's adversity - it is active leadership, because hope is not passive.

Cultural knowledge cycles, accumulates, and shape-shifts through generations, just as water, the transitory element, cycles through the oceans, land and sky. Just as the mighty rivers of the world are the sum of the mountains' trickles, streams, creeks, other rivers and lakes, so too, our global understanding of water can be the joining of diverse cultural streams of thought and perspectives on water management. As the rivers of human knowledge flow across the world's landscapes, a diversity of cultural tributaries interweave, streaming with their own enhancing qualities of clarity, flow, and experiences. Each stream has its own history, flavour and voice, and yet it has the potential to form a larger whole.

Climate change, "it's all about carbon emissions into our atmosphere, right?" "Greenhouse gases", "carbon dioxide", "methane", "carbon credits" and "emission targets"—these familiar phrases encompass the discourse of climate change. Eminent leaders advise: "there's too much carbon, go carbon neutral". But, how does climate change relate to water? Today, how would an indigenous Elder or a Western hydrologist answer the question *What is water*? Furthermore, how would their answers influence how water managers plan to mitigate the challenges of population growth or climate change? I propose we re-examine climate change from a new angle: how would the indigenous perspective on water inform what is happening to the world's water in the context of climate change? The amount of water in the world is constant, although its form, availability, and quality are not. Water is a transformer, a shape-shifter. I submit that the rhythm of water's transformation (phase changes between solid, liquid, and gaseous states) in our world is undergoing a significant change, at a significant rate. Milly *et al.* (2008) observed "substantial anthropogenic change of the Earth's climate is altering the means and extremes of precipitation, evapotranspiration, and rates of discharge of rivers".

So change, in and of itself, is not worrisome. The quickly changing rhythm of water's transformation around the globe is however, the problem. Most critically, humans may be too arrogant, too confident our resilience. If we do not fully understand climate change, do we have time, given the increasing *rate* of change, to adapt our thinking? Climate change has a long history, as some indigenous peoples believe water pre-existed creation when the Earth was dark. The Creator gave us the gift of life and water with the precept that we show respect and restraint.

However, the relatively recent and growing human disrespect for water has lead to our disharmonious earthly existence. Indigenous Elders emphasize the importance of teaching our youth to know and respect water's central spiritual and functional role in our lives. Also, they offer Western science a focusing opportunity: *think of how we treat the water first, since healthy water means a healthy body and ecosystem*.

Water is all around and within us, in an ordinary sense; yet its ubiquity tends us to ambivalence. First Nations have for the most part maintained their reverence for water. Such reverence was once common across cultures in the Western world. Water is the element from which all else came, and therefore it is hypothesized here that water is the primary substance within the interconnected web of life. Water is a meditative medium, a purifier, a source of power, and most importantly it has a spirit. Water is alive – biotic: "Water flows, it is 'living', it moves: it inspires, it heals, it prophesies" (Eliade, 1958).

Elders' identified a fundamental short coming, a flaw in Western science's definition of an ecosystem (Blackstock, 2002). Elders believes, contrary to Western science, that water is alive or biotic – it has a living spirit. Interestingly, however, early Western beliefs of the Greek philosopher Thales, also known as the "Ancient Hydrologist", as he predates Aristotle, asserted water was the origin of all things (Biswas, 1970; Kramer, 1983). He believed that "the earth was created out of the primordial waters of Nun and that such waters were still everywhere below it" (Biswas, 1970). Thales also stated that water is the fundamental, original or primary substance. Greek philosopher Empedocles of Agrigentum postulated the concept of the four basic elements of matter: fire, air, water and earth, which Aristotle later expanded upon by adding a fifth – heaven (Biswas, 1970). So water, originally seemed to have a significant "life giving" importance in Western thought but now is characterized as a disorganized, non-thinking or non-willful particle in the physical world.

Eurocentric thought diverted away from the doctrine of intelligible essences (i.e. spiritual forces, life giving energy or having will) as held now by Algonquian people, or by Ancient Greeks. Water was used in the Old Testament to symbolize cleansing and renewal. British philosophers Thomas Hobbs (1588–1679) and John Stuart Mill (1806–1873), contributed to this diversion away from reverence for water, in the quest to solidify science, in place of religion. Concurrently, although not recognized by Battiste & Henderson, the Protestant Church's reformation may have also contributed to the departure of scientific reason from mysticism. Keith Thomas (1971) examines the Protestant reform of the rituals related to holy water, for instance, as follows: "If the Church's exorcisms and blessings could really work material effects, they argued, then holy water would be the best medicine for any sickness. That this was not the case showed that it was unreasonable and impious to expect God to assist at a ceremony designed to give ordinary water the power to bring health of mind and body, to expel spirits, or drive away pestilence. Holy water, in fact had no more virtue than well-water or river-water". The Protestants preferred to attribute the magical healing properties of holy springs and wells to "natural means".

Vision and Water Cycle
The intent of Blue Ecology's vision is to give priority to water, over humans' financial interests. The highest sustainability test is *water-first*: planned development (e.g. real estate, urban planning, forestry, agriculture, mining, oil and gas extraction) cannot impede the functional delivery of quality water to ecosystems in a healthy rhythm. The five principles of Blue Ecology are:

(a) Spirit: water is a living spirit.
(b) Harmony: harmonious sustainability in a functional rhythm engenders healthy bodies and ecosystems.
(c) Respect: water through ceremony, education and giving

back, else Earth Mother will retaliate by taking water away.

(d) Unity: water has the ability to connect and unify humans because of our common reliance on this basic unit of existence.

(e) Balance: restrained and measured water withdrawals in combination with and giving back (i.e. restoration, monitoring, or ceremony) to watersheds and water.

Hero of Alexandria was a second century BC Greek mathematician and water works engineer. He gave us insight into an archaic view of the hydrological cycle where: "Water also, when consumed by the action of fire, is transformed into air; for the vapour arising from cauldrons placed upon flames is nothing but the evaporation from the liquid passing into air". He characterizes the igneous earth as exhaling dew and warm springs (quoted in Woodcroft, 1851). Hydrologists understanding of the hydrological cycle has now evolved into a more sophisticated model as shown in Oki & Kane's (2006) global cycles or the multilingual depiction on the United States Geological Survey's (2008) website. The hydrological cycle deserves much deeper study and reflection at all educational levels, especially at elementary and high schools. It is critical that there be a universal understanding of water cycles in order to preserve and protect the water on our planet. Indigenous Elders, such as Albert Joseph or the late Mary Thomas, teach that water is our lifeblood, the forest a sponge, and springs a place of spiritual power and clean water. Elders' teachings are summarized in the Blue Ecology water cycle. Five principles of Blue Ecology and water's central spiritual and ecological roles are also represented. This intuitive cycle is meant to exist side-by-side Western science's analytical hydrologic cycle. The *Blue Ecology hydrological cycle* represents some British Columbia indigenous peoples' view of the origin of water, and water's relationship with the four connected worlds (listed in order, from outer to inner circles):

(a) Sky world (i.e. spirit world): The model highlights the

rhythmical role of the sun and moon, and how water is a gift from the spirit world (e.g. creator, god, etc.). Balance and harmony are achieved, through respect, recognition of water's spirit and giving back, as well as by the understanding that all four worlds are connected by water. The moon is not represented in the hydrologic cycle, created by Western Science...why not? The moon influences Earth Mother's rhythm of water.

(b) Earth Mother: All beings on earth are connected to each other by the transitory element, water. Our human health is directly dependent upon the health of the waters that flow through our land and bodies. If the water is sick, so too are we.

(c) Water world: Water has a spirit. Water is always moving and connecting in rhythms. Fish are part of the water, as is all aquatic life, the two are one.

(d) Under world: Water, the lifeblood, seeps, trickles and connects underground, like capillaries under human skin. Water is purified here.

Blue Ecology water cycle and principles

Designed by Michael D. Blackstock. *Blue Ecology Water Cycle:* shows the five principles of Blue Ecology, the moon, sun, and underground capillaries emphasizing connectivity. The cycle treats salt and freshwater as one. This cycle diagram was created and painted by Michael D. Blackstock, and it was first published in a peer-reviewed journal article in 2009 by the International Association of Hydrological Science (see paper at: http://iahs.info/redbooks/a327/iahs_327_0306.pdf). The cycle is meant to be an intuitive companion to Western Science's analytical hydrologic cycle. For instance the moon is represented in this cycle, to capture the rhythms of water.

Now that we have shifted our gaze on climate change to water, let us focus on the language of recent news reports—"melting Arctic ice", "melting permafrost", "raging wildfires", "salt water influx into freshwater aquifers", "receding glaciers", "shifting ocean currents", "drought", "water stress", "higher rainfall", "floods"—and you begin to see the pattern. Climate change is about water and its trends in transformation from one state to another. The sun is the engine of the hydrological cycle; the clouds are the arbiters of energy (Herring, 2002). In the complex, interconnected web of life, Blue Ecology is a means to focus, with new watery eyes, on the current crisis of climate change. A new culture of water is needed in order for humans to adapt. Blue Ecology's philosophy is meant to be the bridge between these two cultural ways of knowing, but given the urgency of climate change, how can Blue Ecology be implemented? First, water needs to be acknowledged by Western science for its central functional and spiritual roles in our world. Recently, the UNESCO-IHP Expert Advisory Group on Water and Cultural Diversity drafted a provisional statement on their definition of water: "the essential lifeblood of our planet with the power to generate, sustain, receive and ultimately, to unify life" (UNESCO-IHP, 2008)[16]. This definition explicitly acknowledges the central functional role of water, which through its movement connects all beings. An exemplar is my re-definition of a forest ecosystem as: "a segment of the landscape, composed of relatively uniform climate, soil, plants, animals, and micro-organisms, which is a community complexly interconnected through a network of freshwater hydrological systems".

Secondly, hydrologists (e.g. water caretakers) could promote, adopt and enshrine global water policy that recognizes a nation's responsibility to take care of the water that travels through, under, over and across its boundaries in a respectful and balanced way. Water caretakers, of all nations, can ensure that current and future generations have certain, unencumbered and predictable access to water. The first question asked when contemplating human development impacts should be: *How does it affect the water?* The highest environmental assessment test for development planning is the water-first principle: planned development (e.g. real estate, urban planning, hydropower, architecture, forestry, agriculture, fishing, aquaculture, mining, oil and gas extraction, etc.) cannot impede the functional delivery of quality water to ecosystems in a healthy rhythm. Water managers, water works engineers, architects and hydrologists could design water works flow to mimic the healthy natural meandering flow of water (see Schwenk, 1996).

Finally, we need to teach children and, for that matter, learn ourselves how to respect and celebrate water's role in our world. Hydrologists are encouraged to embrace the companion Blue Ecology water cycle that is meant to enhance Western science's hydrological cycle by providing a holistic cultural context. Hydrologists and water managers could also communicate complex climate change impacts to the public, using common sense terms. Hydrologists can use the hydrological and Blue Ecology cycles to help explain how and why the climate is changing, since climate change is as much about water, as it is about carbon.

Water is a core human interest. Thirst, *the dry throat*, is a primal experience shared by all beings, and we are unified by our reliance on water. No longer is our goal "sustainable development"—to plan for a high standard of living for our children. Our goal must now be "sustainable survival"—to plan and behave in a cross-culturally collaborative manner that ensures children, generations from now, can survive with dignity in a world where respect for water and our climate is ubiquitous. Global water issues and challenges can be solved because humanity has a collaborative potential that can be mobilized around the common interest of taking care of the water, and because nature is tenacious. There is hope for future generations if we take a water-first approach to setting global priorities.

Blue Ecology, an Attitude Switch

Blue Ecology promotes a new water-first attitude towards water, climate change, and environmental planning. Attitude is *a collection of values, theories, philosophies, beliefs and principles that motivates and influences.*

(Photo by author: Symbolic of human arrogance to control climate)

Water Leadership

Prévoyance: a leadership ability, to prepare for the unexpected, in a world of uncertainty and danger, while maintaining your principles. It is a mindset of learning to make sound judgements over the long run on the basis of imperfect knowledge. The principles of Blue Ecology would be used to make decisions in an uncertain and dangerous world.

(David Hackett Fischer's Champlain's Dream introduced the concept of Prévoyance)

Meanderings

The Meanderings poem and painting below, each speak their own language on water, music, love, and healing. They were inspired, in part, by Thomas Schwenk's book *Sensitive Chaos*. Healthy water meanders across Earth Mother's landscape and through our veins. Healthy water means healthy bodies, mind, spirit and ecosystems. Water's meandering motion occurs within global cycles of rhythm and harmony. In contrast, water forced down a straight-pipe-run erodes noisily and painfully. The duet of music and water in our bones and blood, inspires healing and love. Each elegant liquid-turn flows though channel, vessel and vein, creating healing currents and standing waves, which can trigger the primal memory of love. Nature's inspiration and the musician's harmonics travels faster through water. The painter, poet, musician and essayist in joint performance can reach new audiences who are keen with eyes to see the unifying potential of water and ears to hear the spirit and harmony of water's flow. I wrote the poem *Meanderings* to be accompanied by the wonderful pianist Serge Mazerand, and the painting is the result of collaboration with the talented painter Annerose Georgeson.[2] We exercise the collaborative potential of music and art into the mainstream discourse on water, the environment and sustainability. You can listen to this poem at http://sergemazerand.com/recordings/healing-music/ .

---

[2] The word Oceaness is credited to Serge Mazerand, who titled a CD he recorded "Oceaness". It means an ocean of endless possibilities.

From sky-blue eyes and silky veins and love to be
Water flows through my mind like a melody
Though, it's hard to explain this music to somebody
Note by note, drops drip into streams of harmony

Up and back and buSted-down
We've rid this river, rou-nd and round
High and low and through Rough-waters
You and I and love, are all that matters

In a sma-ll moment, do you recall how it all inno-cently began?
Falling through the calm, a wide-snowflake or a first rain drop
Dri--p^-drop^, Dri--p^-drop^, Dri--p^-drop^: Dri--p^-drop^
Li-quid trickles, Li-quid trickles, Li-quid trickles: Li--quid tri-ckles

Up and back and buSted-down
We've rid this river, rou-nd and round
High and low and through Rough-waters
You and I and love, are all that matters

Drops drip into trickles and riVers breeeeathing streams
We're caught-up in this current, flasHing by in dreams
Gurgle'n mur---mur, Gurgle'n mur---mur; Gurgle'n murmurin'
Babbles'n burblin' Babbles'n burblin': Baaaa-bbles'n burrrrblin'

Up and back and buSted-down
We've rid this river, rou-nd and round
High and low and through Rough-waters
You and I and love, are all that matters

Whirrrrrlin' whirlpools are givin' me a dizzy spell
Tightly twistin' coils pulsating and interplaying well
Meandering currents tracing across silt and sand
Ripples purl and waves curl over contours of your land

Up and back and buSted-down
We've rid this river, rou-nd and round
High and low and through Rough-waters
You and I and love, are all that matters

As quick as it comes – the quick it flows into lakes
Steel yourself before gravity pulls and takes
Lap'n-ripple, sLap'n-ripple, Lap'n-ripple a little more
Slipping, sli-pping down; cascading into din and roar

Up and back and buSted-down
We've rid this river, rou-nd and round
High and low and through Rough-waters
You and I and love, are all that matters

Its raining on our river again; river is flood-high and risin'
We're runnin' swift in white-water; its raining again
Boil'n swell, Boil'n swell, dancing among passion splashes
Whoosh'n-crash, Crash'n-Whoosh': Whooooosh'n-crashes

Up and back and buSted-down
We've rid this river, rou-nd and round
High and low and through Rough-waters
You and I and love, are all that matters

Our river's surrenderin' to the salty taste of turquoise sea
We're bobbin' under noon sun, meandering with Blue Ecology
Come on honey, let's rock and loll to a drizzlin' beat
Hiss'n whistle we are vapourin' in this sizzlin' heat

Up and back and buSted-down
We've rid this river, rou-nd and round
High and low and through Rough-waters
You and I and love, are all that matters

Water in my red seas sings love and pain and sweet summer rain
Music heals and tunes my cells, by rippling thru my veins
To oceaness music, I sing a million words, two by two
Showering down from me to you, and they all mean *I love you*

Blue Ecology: a collaborative acrylic painting
by Michael D. Blackstock and Annerose Georgeson.

AC DC's Climate Change Prophecy

Four bells tolling
Dong, Dong, Dong, Dong

I'm a rolling thunder, a pouring rain
Climate Change I am a comin' on like a hurricane
My lightning's flashing across the sky
You're only young but you're gonna die

I won't take no prisoners, won't spare no lives
Some are denying, nobody's putting up a fight
I got my bell, I'm gonna take you to hell
I'm gonna get you, *Carbon-Satan* get you

Hell's bells
Yeah, hell's bells
You got me ringing hell's bells
My temperature's high, hell's bells

I'll give you black sensations up and down your spine
If you're into evil you're a friend of mine
See the white light flashing, *blue ice melting*
'Cause if good's on the left,
Then I'm stickin' to the right

I won't take no prisoners, won't spare no lives
Nobody's puttin' up a fight
I got my bell, I'm gonna take you to hell
I'm gonna get you, *Carbon-Satan* get you
Hell's bells...[1]

Words in italics are my additions to AC DC's classic song *Hells Bells*. They added the sound of the bell tolling to the beginning as tribute to Bon Scott.

Birth-Normal

It's hard to know what the hell is going on out there!

If you were born into a world of 10,000 orcas dressed in *robe bleu*...that would be your birth-normal state. But sadly, if you were born into a world of 75 propeller-scraped orcas (make that 74, as J50 just passed away) ...that would be your birth-normal state. You would not know any better. This is one of the biggest philosophical and rhetorical challenges facing the discourse of environmental change.

Daniel Pauly saw a shifting baseline while he watched the fish disappear. How many sockeye traveled the Fraser River 500 years ago?

The syndrome is created when our "normal" baseline view of the world is anchored or imprinted at birth. Rather than a view of the landscape in it's untouched state, that once was.

Go to http://world.time.com/timelapse2/ to see how your neighbourhood, your land has changed.

Anthropomorphism

noun: **anthropomorphism**

        1.   the attribution of human characteristics or behavior to a god, animal, or object.

I remember, standing with a group of my son's classmates, while we watched a fisheries biologist dissect a sockeye salmon, along the bank of the Adams River. A child asked "How do they know when and how to come here? They must be smart", she said. The biologist replied, "salmon can't think or feel, they come here using instinct – it's hard wired into them."

My Gitxsan teachings say salmon are people, and they can transform from fish to human form when they enter their world.

Anthropomorphism is a means for humans to rationalize the destruction of animal and fish habitat - salmon can't feel sadness, they have no will, they can't think. Therefore they feel no grief when we destroy their home. Wrong.

Anthropomorphism is a flawed assumption of science-based environmental planning. Assumptions are like rust, they will eventually sink your ship. Let's stop teaching our children this terrible concept. Rather, let's teach children that animals and fish can think, can feel and they have a will.

Turrets and Florets

Rolling Moon edged up Marble Canyon's limestone mountain-side. Coyote and Raven had their backs into it, pushing their silver bangle. "Use a little elbow grease Coyote", Raven chortled. They pushed by the budworm riddled Douglas-fir trees, which were knuckled into the steep pinegrass slope. Halfway, they became thirsty, stopped, and went to a nearby solitary turret of carbonate precipitate nestled in the grassland, called Soda Spring. They made this secret spring, long ago, by pushing a thin strand of lava rock up to the surface, and then sucked water up the artery, using a tule reed. Coyote carved a protective rock-lid for the spring-water-rock-bowl. People come here to pray, heal, and purify. Tonight these two tricksters were just thirsty. Raven lifted the lid off and sipped bubbly ochre-tinted water; Coyote watched the lifeblood, in the spring-bowl, pulse to the rhythm of Earth Mother's heartbeat. Before returning to their nighttime job, they left tobacco, to thank her. As they returned to the moon, Coyote told Raven how much he relished the sound of rain falling on the grass, "it makes a jingle, jingle, jingle sound, and from now on, our dancers will wear bells to honour the rain!" he announced.

Coyote and Raven finally settled the teetering moon on the horizon, balanced between earth and sky. Atop Chimney Rock, legs dangling, they gazed into the pellucid depths of Pavilion Lake. "Do you hear the clouds talking?" asked Raven. They saw a lingering ripple on the still lake, left by the lanky tail of Eep, the mysterious lake dweller. The travelling wave rocked yodeling loons as it passed under, and tremolos crescendoed. These throat singers gathered after their nightly visit and work-bee, as their kids awoke in the reeds.

Raven and Coyote were very tired now, because they had spent the previous summer's day, having too much fun. They chased darting turquoise damselflies among tule and horsetail reeds: damsels in singles and soaring couplets, just above lime-jade waters, dappled with sun-white diamond sparkles. First damselflies grace the lake, next comes the dragonflies to the race. Each time either Raven or Coyote met a beautiful woman, they would create a damselfly in her memory, and let her live at Pavilion Lake.

Pavilion Lake has been Raven's and Coyote's touchstone playground, since time beyond time, as long as the Secwepemc and St'at'imc people can remember. Remember, Coyote reminisced, "Elders would joke, the lake is alive, it farts like a skunk."

Raven had stolen a turquoise paint powder from the Chief-of-the-Skies and sprinkled it in the lake, painting it a clear blue in the middle, with a line of turquoise along the shores . While Coyote made his mark on the lake, by teaching the Little People, who lived in karst caves, to transform into loons at night, so they could swim to the bottom and make hobbit-like limestone coral carvings and microbialite sculptures. Coyote sucked spring water up through reeds to fill the lake, and then Coyote provided the Little People with tiny magnetic animals to help re-shape the ancient coral debitage back into its microbialite turrets and florets. The magical mixture of sacred water and primordial limestone became the Little Peoples' artist palette. To protect their sacred spot, Raven and   Coyote placed guards at each end of the lake. Kingfisher, the powerful transformer who could travel in air and water worlds, guarded the west end, while Osprey was posted on the Romanesque coastal power-pole-tower at the east end. At night, bats emerged on aerial patrol. In day, Ant Lions hid in the sand, among prickly pear cactus, to protect the surrounding forests, like Apache warriors hidden in the desert. Mickey and the Pavilion Queen patrolled shores for forest fires, while the Lady of the Lake serenaded, playing her ghost-guitar.

But, was this enough to protect the lake? Was It enough to buffer it from man's increasingly disrespectful *sea-dooish* behavior? No, humans had to change their attitude towards water, by learning about Blue Ecology's principles. So Raven and Coyote sowed seeds of ideas in the people who visited, to teach them, through beauty, that water is alive, and needs to be shown due respect. Raven and Coyote had most faith in the children that visited the lake: they intuitively understand how precious Pavilion Lake is, and thus would become guardians and caretakers of the lake, like Kingfisher and Osprey.

The moon rolled over and faded into the rising sunlight; the lake she gave a breath and made a cloud in the morning sky, which rose heaven's high. Coyote, caught a glimpse with the tail of his eye, and said: "I wonder, it may be fun to bring astronauts here to work and play, they have seen the earth from the moon, and will know that Pavilion is the crown jewel on the blue marble." Coyote replied: "Yeah, the sky is *not* the limit, dream big my friend. *Sic parvis magna.*"[3]

---

[3] This story, is my from imagination, and is not an oral history from a particular First Nation. My son David imagines loons drink a little water, and hold it in their throat to make different calls and songs. The "sky is not the limit" phrase is used by Canadian astronaut, Chris Hadfield, whom we met at Pavilion Lake during the summer of 2010, while he was participating in the NASA/CSA space analogue project. Wonderous and humbling views of earth can be found at:
http://earthobservatory.nasa.gov/IOTD/view.php?id=46820.

Raven flies high with the satellites watching the Nile's firefly-like lights spill forth into the Mediterranean's night of darkness.

Falco and Odonata

Speed, aerobatics and legerity define their grace
Each the fastest dare-devils of their flighted-race
Winged shadow-forms flicker and flow along
Triggering their preys' meadow warning song

Both falcons and dragonflies claim the skies
Acrobatic flight, spins, soars and stoop-dives Zig-
zag, stop-start hovers and backward glides Each
faster than a waaaster, feared by all sides

Falcons are protectors of fresh air skies
Fresh water is watched over by dragonflies
Sadly, both stewards exchange snarl-words
Since time in memorial, each crossed swords

That was, until Falco and Odonata redefined the gag
Kids taking the age-old test of falcon-dragonfly tag
Odonata, striking electric blue, basked on an aspen to rest
Falco, impressing parents watching from cliff-edge nest

Wind hissed behind Falco's fastest dive, he surely could not miss
Odonata's eyes notice tracking shadow lept from dawn bliss
She darted, dashed and dodged into prickly thistles
Falco surprised, eased up his dive with a brake-whistle

His beak, a fletched arrow, closing upon her svelte abdomen
She swerved, weaved and ducked just as he struck, and then;
Falco's prize tail feather caught loose on a thistle-spine
Tho' he nicked a gash along Odonata's forward wing line

Falco had not earned the avian-hunter's moustache
Odonata had failed her insect-kind's peregrine dash
Falco's stoops and rolls were now wonky and poppy
Odonata's hovering and darts, well, were quite sloppy

One day, under the blue dome, while sky-patrolling
Falco spied a black cloud billowing, smog-choking
Odonata too, surveying a creek, saw an oily rainbow-sheen
Spillage on water, sliming homewards to ponds downstream

Both flew back to their flock and swarm to warn
But, ignored they were, as we know was the norm
Mouse woman noticed water's strange taste and algal bloom
Pekid falcons and dragonflies limp, signaled ecological gloom

Mouse Woman, using a comet's tail, restored Falco's plume
Spider-Mother's silk thread to mend Odonata's wing wound
Mouse Woman announced they now are the fastest repair-pair
Their mission to plant horsetail, which cleanses water and air

Falco and Odonata flew hither and yon, to creeks and lakes
Purr-words 'tween enemies of old; strong allies they do make
Mouse Woman now less worried, its not too late
Falcon and dragonfly averted a near certain fate.

Sockeye Salute, Ode and Elegy

A duo of silvery-red rain descendants
Ancient blazing downpour remnants

We two share-a-glance askance smelling sweet sad words
Liquid lenses' tenacious muscling rhythms side and forward

Our gestural acknowledgment welcomes ancestors
Drumming and singing; four races, brothers and sisters

With our own plan, we keep knowledge in our own way
We can assure you, your experts have gone astray

Welling familiar in home water's cool touch moist
Flowforms stirring crimson, algae-green and turquoise

Currents blending bubbles painting a reddish modello
Riverine art drifts and swirls, lingering sunset-yellow

We meet the translucent Pacific Salmon Thinker's eyes
Contrapposto atop his petroglyph poem shored wise

His tears glinting in the burn of fall, mixing with our own
He welcomes our old life to the river rocks of home

Our guardian brother is saddened aloud
His people's wasting ways, the madding crowd

He, side-by-side our ancestors, pleads to global travelers
 Respect us, the everlasting-silvery swimmers
 Respect the waters we bless
 Else, we fear the worst.
 Now, go home with vivid passion
 Entreat the change,
 your heart and soul knows urgent and best.

Adams River Sockeye (painting by author)

Rivers Reach the Sea

In the beginning the clean rains came down
A welcomed pitter-pattering, drip-drop sound
Rain began an infinite task of painting
Pale parched land, glossy and glistening
Fresh mountain airs inflate me
Mossy trickles emerge from trees
Always going to where I'm coming from
Swirl with gravity girl, fueled by the sun

> *There's a lot of work to do*
> *Flowing from here to you*
> *Trickle, ripple, rumble, roar*
> *I just don't know if I can do it anymore*

They use me, waste me; disrespect and disgrace me
Common sense isn't as common, as it used to be
I work all day flowing to a distant shore
Eating up meters, my back is getting sore
I'll tell you what, I'll share a thing or two, with you
City folk, country too, can't recall what I was meant to do
It's lonely without my silvery-swimmer friends
The sea-breeze told me, they'll not return again

> *There's a lot of work to do*
> *Flowing from here to you*
> *Trickle, ripple, rumble, roar*
> *I just don't know if I can do it, anymore*

Are you listening, do you hear the polluted rains?
Are you watching, to see me, the vacant river's pain
I meander, stretch and dream, with tenacity
I need your help, to make sure that I reach the sea

> *There's a lot of work to do*
> *Flowing from here to you*
> *Trickle, ripple, rumble, roar*
> *I just don't know if I can do it, alone, anymore*

Water and Music

Water and music, the twinning, is a healing gurgling spring. Your body is mostly water, and the proportion varies between 62-78% depending on age and gender. While at the Science Museum in London, England, in 2008, with my family, I played with an interactive demonstration of how a standing wave, in an enclosed glass tube of water, can be created by varying the frequency and amplitude of sound. I was struck visually by the effect of sound on water. Water is more sensitive to sound than air, and sound travels about four times faster in water. I wondered, in the museum, if music could sculpt or mold human cell structure? Furthermore, the combination of frequency and amplitude, in a natural harmonic way, in a musical way, could assist the healing of our body's cells. Remember when you heard a song that struck a chord with you, and you felt get-up-and-dance-happy, peaceful, or even sad? It just happens naturally, unforced. Your cells, and water within the cell, respond to certain musical vibrations, phrases, or patterns, in a way that could possibly promote healing. Following this line of reason, sounds outside of our natural hearing range may be able affect our body. Perhaps, our watery-cell's heightened ability to "hear or sense" sound outside of our ears' range is our sixth sense? A type of weak signal detection; we are not trained to pay attention to or honour. We can learn to *tune in*, and select music that creates certain waves in the water of our cells. At first, the sounds may be like co-mingling radio stations, but we can learn to become discerning. As if you are listening to one radio station, as another fades in and out, and your brain tries to focus on the apparently ineffable.

From a Blue Ecology perspective, what if we studied the health of our bodies, and spirit, from a water-first perspective? Consequently, our first health diagnostic questions would be: Is de-hydration a possible cause of a symptom? In particular, the brain has a very high relative proportion of water, as compared to the rest of our body. Is our mood associated with our level of hydration? Let's consider alcohol, for instance, as a de-hydration vector, how does that affect our mood? If we are well hydrated can we potentially "feel" (i.e. sympathetic vibration) and enjoy music more fully, and become more intuitive? This thinking is related to the field of harmonic healing for sure, but is much broader because water is always moving and connects us directly to earth and her spirit.

Blue Ecology Boy created by Michael Blackstock for the "Blank Boy" exhibits founded by Danny Yung

Ice Talking

Winter's sting-chillness crept back from morning light
Sky giants drilling holes in the frozen sky making bright
Warming lake ice sings: Plue-oooop, *Twoong T^ooonk*
Water giant awakens, she shifts noticing the warmth long
Her water-bones cracked
Aches soothed in her limnological back
She hears falling snow on water

Bones and Blood

I was born and raised with music in my water
O water! Where art thou?
I thirst for you
O music! Where art thou?
I thirst for you
Water records music in my soul
Bones and blood
Bones and blood
Water's both love and pain
And sweet summer rain
O Brothers and Mothers let's go down to the river
And see if there is any water today

Dust before Dawn

Dust before dawn
Thirst in the night
Pray and sing
For the rain
To splash this thirsty land

She prepares her children to bring rain
And her tears to be liquid melody
A light breath arose from her
And became a cloud
The rain came beautifully
Jingling on the grass
Our rain-bath in dusted nakedness
Rain is a symbol of mercy in the desert
Pepper in the eyes of the Devil
Send out a Raven
Scout
Rain shower
Just made the heat wet

Drink-a-watta

A tall drink-a-watta on a hot afternoon
Taste dust, fine cinnamon dust
There's Gotta-be-watta, gotta find it soon
Quench my thirst, it's a longing must

Sitting pretty, a tall drink-a-watta drifts in the sky
Taughtin' she winked and blew the other waaay
Shimmering with hope, a dry river bed
A mirage turned to dust, then dried dead

> *I wanna drink-a-watta, watta*
> *It's a cooker out today*
> *gotta have a cooool drink-a-watta*
> *heat's bitter-sweetness iZ here-ta-stay*

Dusty tongue searches the sky
Hunting for moista, hidden away
Coaxing a flush of rain
To wet a cracking pain

My thirst just won't go away
A tall drink-a-watta would hit the spot
It's gettin' hotta would'nt you say?
Pray to the rain gods, untwist this manila knot

> *I wanna drink-a-watta, watta*
> *It's a cooker out today*
> *gotta have a cooool drink-a-watta*
> *heat's bitter-sweetness iZ here-ta-stay*

Field Identification Guide to Life

Table of Contents

Chapter One

Chapter Two

Chapter Three

Chapter Four

Epilogue

Gravity: A Thought Experiment

A person is most likely to be situated, in the future, where they currently rest in space, because gravity determines it so. Why? It's the simplest way.

Life is about negotiating with gravity to release it's grip - wrestling with static motion. Gravity is always looking for a foothold, a flaw to dig it's claws.

A thought experiment: stand at the railway station's platform. Wait for a train to take you away. The change-train arrives as the clock strikes a crisis. Einstein is the conductor. The shortest distance between two stations is time.

Ant logic is two dimensional. Wobbly particles journey map pattern is not transect. Ants' search pattern is wiggly wobbly.

I once figured out the meaning of life, exhilarated I feel asleep. Regretfully, I didn't write my epiphany down, because I forgot it when I awoke. Everything is fleeting and temporary.

What is the happiest thought of your life?

Wyget's Quips

You can bring one thing back from each dream.
Intuition is dream recall.
Shoot the shit, shoot the breeze.
He was the right tool for the job.
He could talk the paint off floor.
Chataway getaway thataway.
That dog barked all night until I was blue in the face.
Do you question answers or answer questions?
Time won't wait for you to make a decision.
There is a disturbance in the texture of this poem.
I risk my fears, I make myself mad.
You are always going to where you are coming from.
The wind was drunk.
Just talking about thirst, makes me thirsty.
Don't panic, I've got bannock.
We're **3** bad decisions from pushing a shopping cart.
If they are repeating themselves, they are unheard.
My conscience spanked me.
The long way around is closer to home.
It's an Old Indian('s) trick.
He was praying at the Church of Last Resort.
Common sense isn't that common.
Love triumphs over gossip.
Women knit words, men tink words.
Flowing water makes secret conversations safe.
When water decreases, ants eat fish.
When water increases, fish eat ants.
When all was said and done,
more was said than done
I am the curator of my brain.
You can't fix lazy

Wyget is the Gitxsan trickster character, Raven.

Honey and Her Sting

She takes a lover, like her baths
When I need or want one, she laughs

Honey and bumble bees a-stewing
Lust for honey blinds her lovers to her sting

Raven's silhouette fleets across harvest moon
A new lover's thunderhead rolls in to croon

Sheet swimmers' tongues lick lips
Hands grasp on hips

Each other plays their lover's ding-a-ling
Chuck Berry rocks her cherry to sing

Swoons and gasps, more like yells
Ignite the loon song, passion swells

Fire the cannon, orgasm in a lightning storm
A rain-bath washes the naked warm

All her life, coldy and sadly
 She waited, days went by
She who dreamed wildly and madly
 Has feasted now, happy to die[5]

---

[5]First verse was inspired by a newspaper op-ed column I half remember written by Heather Mallick, about older women and their approach to lovers. Last verse inspired by a poem by Emily Georgiana, Countess of Winchilsea (1850).

Winter Cold and Cabin Heat

She carried the clam shell, protecting her fire-ember
Husband broke trail, November and most of December
As night's ice fog settles, they open the cabin door
Both flopped, gaily exhausted, onto pine plank floor
Rusty bolts and frayed rope
Windy gusts snowed-up window frames
Frosted feather patterns fanned out on the panes
She lit a fire with her ember, their fingers benumbed
Smoky coffee smells in late December
Crackling firewood, sparking cast-iron echoes
Tickling the sting of winter's chillness, the fire glows

> *She lured and invited him*
> *Your hug feels like home*
> *Close the door, crack a window*
> *I've a hunch its goin'-a-git*
> *hot in here tonight*

To give pleasure is to gain it
Her nighty rucked up tall
Her heart pinned to the wall
Her hand grasps the window sill
Her tongue slides melts window's ice
Her passion-path chronicles allegretto
Whence, suddenly her fingers scrape
Ice curls, furls under nail's plate
Outside the snow scrubbed the earth
Rivers merged and drank their troubles away
Breaths made too much noise in the stillness
They lay spawned out

> *She lured and invited him*
> *Your hug feels like home*
> *Close the door, crack a window*
> *I've a hunch its goin'-a-git*
> *hot in here tonight*

Ursala and the Orange

A smile across a fuliginous crowd
A love between strangers, fundamentally not allowed
He shoulders his way; vibrations before she was fully aware
His precious orange, to the girl with the carrot-red hair.

This rare fruit's glow brightened the village's umbra and nooks
Her breath in the stillness of the Great War's smoked air
Freckled teenager and forbidden soldier exchanged liquid looks
A citrus-breeze swirls her virescent scarf and curls of hair.

A *tableau vivant* to her starving belly, whole-orange-love
Hours stacked upon days, which flashed by like a dove
Until, what was meant to be, happened to be.
He whispered: "The orange was to be eaten, don't you see?"
She says: "Oh, but I have been, and now I will share with thee."

The Blind Florist

Nydia often says, "Reality is for those who lack imagination."

Her florist's hands were spellbinding, as they moved through the air with spark and zing, painting fragrant floral notes. Each flower has an energetic vibration and a precise fluidity of expression. She arranges flowers to entice people to surrender to the bouquet's flow. Fresh flowers especially exuded the energy she smells for, plans for.   Bees know.

Nydia loved violets (*Viloaceae*). The soundtrack *La Violetera* by Jose Padilla, pulls tears from her eyes. The Greek word for violet is *Io*, the daughter of King Argos. Zeus loved her. However, Zeus was concerned that Hera would discover their illicit affair, so he turned Io into a heifer and then he created the sweet-scented flowers we now know as violets for her to eat. The scent of violets was also the favorite perfume of Josephine Bonaparte. When Napoleon returned from banishment in Elba, Josephine was dead. He picked a bouquet of violets for her grave. When Napoleon died, violets and a lock of Josephine's hair were found in a locket.

One of Nydia's favourite movies, not surprisingly, is *Scent of a Woman* (1971). The main character is a blind man, Vittorio Gassman, played exceptionally well by Al Pacino. Vittorio said, "One is so lucky to be blind because blind people don't see things as they are, but as how they imagine them to be." Nydia was blinded at the age of ten while helping her Grandmother make ice cream. She used lye (caustic soda) to thicken the ice cream. It has an exothermic reaction with tears, and heat is liberated. Like Helen Keller, as a child, Nydia too found joy in the garden, as she felt along the square stiff boxwood (*Buxaceae*) hedges. Guided by the sense of smell, she discovered spring's first violets and lilies (*Liliaceae*). She found comfort in the coolness of leaves and grass, hiding her hot, healing face, and newly darkened eyes.

In floral design, details are not minutiae to Nydia; they are central, foundational chunks of important ambience. They are as big a hot air balloons, not ant-sized bits, not nuisances underfoot. A completed picture is made of perfumed puzzle pieces; these puzzle-stalks are not details, they are the bouquet. Women know that both safety and sensuality are born from details. God(dess) is in the details. Though, in the end, she bows to natural forces, her friends like to say *when it happens...it was meant to be*. A natural forces' approach is one of humility and surrendering to Nature. Human's arrogance blinds them to the natural forces of beauty and synchronicity. Though, it is folly to rely on luck alone, it is wise to invest in preparation, hence the details.

A tiny four-chairs-and-a-table central courtyard is her safe spot, in her home, at the rear of the flower shop, located along Fort Street, in Victoria, British Columbia. Rough old ships-ballast brick walls frame her moon garden, festooned with Angel's Trumpet (*Brugmansia*), Jasmine of the Night (*Cestrum nocturnum*), and night blooming Cereus (*Epiphyllum oxypetallum)*. The Moonflower (*Ipomoea alba*) climbs the scraping brick, it is a flowering vine with large heart-shaped leaves framing fragrant white flowers. Opening at dusk and lasting until morning, the Moonflower resembles its relative the Morning Glory (*Ipomoea*). The most pleasant and intense production of odor by flowering plants comes with night blooming flowers. These attract pollinators by scent rather than sight; they are much more fragrant than flowers that use color.

Her custom sculpted soapstone lounge-chair, a seated water fountain, rests in room's centre. Her place had a smell of recent rain, old books, grass, with a tang of acidity and a hint of vanilla. In the corner stood a replica of Randolf Rogers' evocative marble sculpture of the Blind Flower Girl of Pompeii – gesturing with a hand to her ear, to hear the goings-on.

"What bouquet messages, flower passages, should I arrange for my dinner?" pondered Nydia to herself. "I shall imagine I am in Constantinople during the 17th century where floriography, the secret language of flowers, first took root. Illiterate concubines communicated in code to each other, using flower arrangements."

The American poet and botanist James Gates Percival wrote a poem entitled "Language of Flowers", and one line summed it up for Nydia: *In Eastern lands they talk in flow'rs.*

Flowing water gently massaged her tense shoulders, while she sat naked on her soapstone water-throne. Her dinner guests were just settling. Magic is about to happen in this room, and it happens on its own. Nydia blinks, taking dream photographs, *tableau vivants*, to document the night. She charms her two guests, a couple, Carmencita and Jasper. Charm is getting a 'yes' without asking the question. Gratitude, shall reseat itself tonight as the couple has agreed on a way to thank Nydia for her truly exceptional talents. *Scentless Apprentice* by Nirvana (inspired by Patrick Suskind's book *Perfume*) echoed in the room. "Jasper, now please provide me with a review of Carmencita's outfit, before I totally dim the lights (...it was always night for her)," Nydia asked.

"Carmencita is a composed feminine masterpiece. Describing her is an exercise in negative space; it is what she is not wearing, more than wearing. Simply put, she is wearing a fuchia coloured, low cut, short dress. It has a tear drop opening cut on each side that visibly accentuates her waist and ribs. Her wonderfully wavy black hair is let down, and swept to one side, coyly hiding her left blue eye. Besides her dress, and her black pumps, she is, as far as I can tell, wearing nothing else. There are obvious clues to this effect, and I will leave that to your imagination," said Jasper. Carmencita giggled.

Nydia's free flow guided her guests, "Let's all dine on a plated feast of senses, starting with my Luciferin bisque (light-bringer) made from freshwater snails (*Latia neritodes*) and Bitter Oyster mushrooms (*Panellus stipticus*). Bioluminescent Avatar-like nanoparticles will soup your veins, while you dine in mystery. What we hear will inform our taste (in the background music from *The Piano* soundtrack foreshadows a Holly-Hunter-sizzle). We resolve our sense into five flavour dimensions (sour, sweet, salty, bitter and umami). Higher pitches emphasize sweeter flavours, while lower tones underline notes of bitterness. Notice how your tongue curls upward for sweeter tastes and downward to expel bitter food."   Jasper and Carmencita's palates traveled cleft and score. Nydia finished her soup, and picked up where she left, "Charles Spence, a renowned Oxford psychologist, conducted an experiment at the famous Spanish estaurant *El Bulli*, where the diners rated strawberry mousse 10 percent sweeter and 15 percent more flavourful when served on white plates. Other diners find seafood flavours stronger when they hear the sound of the ocean, for instance. Sense of touch is enjoyed all over our bodies. Michelangelo's insight: *to touch can be to give life. Oo la la*, don't get me started on the study of hedonics and floriography, I am so passionate about composing sensual our state-of-consciousness meals. Do you notice the warmth of excitation stirring in your blood?"

Now, desert for two. Centered on the courtyard table sat a chilled ceramic dish full of deep-dark chocolate ice cream, garnished with the flowers of Blue Pea (*Clitoria ternatea*), and paired with Summerhill Pyramid's ice wine, from the verdant Okanagan Valley. There were no spoons. There were no wine glasses. Frisson's shudder-travels down Nydia's bare spine, "I surrender to you both," she announced. As if on a conductor's cue, the playlist's needle landed on *La Puerta de Vino: Wine Gate (to Alhambra palace)* by Debussy. The three got lit.

Nydia emitted, "We are free fireflies, smelling the darkness of light! Carmencita, drink drops of wine perched on my glowing petals; Jasper, enjoy my chocolate-sundae-breasts." His fingers exciting blue light from Nydia's pleasuredomes. Carmencita's tongue dances along Nydia's long blooming flower, pink in bud and open creamy white.

Nydia sees a Vesuvius-like exploded star bloom, a cosmic flower. A warm glow ensued, a warm flow dissolved her muscles like butter. She hung wet words on the line to dry.

Sometimes

Sometimes you know
Sometimes you don't know
When...it's the last time you will:
        See him
        See her
            Eat that food
            Sit in your
            favourite chair
                Smell a smell
                Hear her laugh
                Feel his skin
        Touch her
                Kiss her
                Shake his hand
        Walk that peaceful trail
        Eat at your favourite restaurant
            Drive there
            Pet your dog
            Cuddle your cat
            Ride your horse
            Kick that ball
            Eat bacon
        See the dimple on your child's hand
        Sleep with your baby
        Hear your son's voice, before it changes

Hurry

If you are in such a fucking hurry
You should have left yesterday.

...Better right than fast

School Yard Buzz

Hark, bees and bees
There's a new buzz in
      the tiny old Pritchard school house
      if you please.
A nostalgic buzz *IZZZ* about the yard.
A September-busy-bee buzz and bustle.
Bees laze lazy during summer daze.
Winter's nipping them in the bum, bee be busy.

Just like before, when the
      first coat of paint went on the front door
      blackboard was midnight black
      children's buzz settling in before the bell
      teacher writing out the lesson plan for the day.
That bustle has been replaced by a
      behind-the-blackboard-buzz.
An old dark-honey hive is entombed
      in walls of education.
Healthy strong queens are now produced
      in place of scholars.
Dark honey of aspen, ponderosa pine, fireweed,
      blueberries and school-yard dandelions.
There's a story in this honey
      that tastes of brown sugar on a summer's day.[6]

---

[6] Rudyard Kipling's "The Bee-Boy's Song" is an inspiration for the first verse.

Bumble bee painting by author.

Top Kill Oil Spill

Eleven souls drift in oil plumes
Robots cutin' a blow-out preventer in the gloom
Sparks and spirits swirlin' around Davey Jones' locker
Just BP patient, we don't know how to stop'er
Gas phantoms circle, while robot's blades spin
Way down at the Deepwater horizon, in the din
Forty two days on now, at about 1472 meters down
Live video feeds the dead to the hapless Crown

> *Top kill oil spill washed down onto Louisiana*
> *Slick's just about a mile from TexarKana*
> *In the Gulf, golf balls, oil and oil booms*
> *This damn leak ain't goin' nowhere soon*

BP's plan A, gave way to B, C, D and E
Oil, smoke and dispersant travel the sea
Pledges and promises give way to skimming and burning
Cajun shrimp fade, replaced by fisher's yearning
Ocean's blue ecology stained by crude technology
BP's reputation, stained by a naïve ideology
This oil may seem, a drop in the bucket
But this drunk's not hit rock bottom yet

> *Top kill oil spill washed down onto Louisiana*
> *Slick's just about a mile from TexarKana*
> *In the Gulf, golf balls, oil and oil booms*
> *This damn leak ain't goin' nowhere soon*

New Orleans is sinking again
How are the fish goin' to win?
Zyedco and Texaco, uptown and downtown
We need to all pitch in, or we all fall down

Chaos and Desire

Johnny Credit and the Cards
Sing love and lust are at eternal odds
Headliners at Club Chaos and Desire
Passion trade winds fan alcohol fire

Things are a little haywire
Here at Club Chaos and Desire
Johnny will lend you all his money
At 20 percent interest, that is, honey

> *Things around here are not quite right*
> *Tides not come in for the second night*
> *Guys sporting tattoos and snowshoes*
> *Gals wearing lace long johns and stilettos*

Bartender serves humid and turbulent booze
A toque-hair seismic-chick cuts recklessly loose
Each gal has an ironside,
I prefer their sunny-side

Raven's spying eyes have crow's feet
Coyote just stole the drummer's beat
My heart spins east, my head goes west
Isn't that Grace Kelly in a strapless dress?

> *Things around here are not quite right*
> *Tides not come in for the second night*
> *Guys sporting tattoos and snowshoes*
> *Gals wearing lace long johns and stilettos*

Inspired by my favourite thriller movies: Manon Briand's (2002) "Chaos and Desire" and Alfred Hitchcock's (1954) "Rear Window".

She's listening to music about Chaos and Desire
Flying on the creative wings of Cupid's choir
Intimate love inspires feminine-flows of Aphrodite
Pleased by Voluptas, daughter of Eros and Psyche

> *Things around here are not quite right*
> *Tides not come in for the second night*
> *Guys sporting tattoos and snowshoes*
> *Gals wearing lace long johns and stilettos*

Where am I?

Lookin'
politically correct
department store advertising-
flyers
photos of Black, White, and Asian kids
modellin' their new school clothes.
Where am I?
If I close one eye, and squint the other eye
the Asian kid kinda looks like my cousin Cyril Sam.
Where are the aboriginal kids?
Am I invisible, am I too poor to shop; or
am I not a politically correct image?
Is there still racism?
Why don't the Black and Asian kids
say somethin' on my behalf?
They know what it is like.[8]
Shannen's dream
should come true.[9]

---

[8] A collage art work was done by the author using advertising flyers to highlight this theme.
[9] See   http://www.fncfcs.com/shannensdream/

Water Equations

Water (liquid)	=	f(water)
Water (steam)	=	f(fire)
Water (ice)	=	f(earth)
Water (fog)	=	f(air)
Weather	=	f(water's mood)

Merge and exit mathematics is for open systems.

A whole systems approach is to balance equations as a function of the harmonious flow into and out of categories.

Tree Coral: Pavilion Lake microbialite photo (author), on a fir tree.

Moose Horns and Pine Cones

If a cone is on a spruce tree,
        what do you call it?
If antlers are on a moose
        what do you call them?[10]

Lance Bearing

Mosquitoes lance beared
Rode atop horseflys heralded
Bach's bees' xylophones

Stellar Steller's Jay

What? I see you, hopping on my deck chair chattin'-
    away, peering in my window.
Come to visit, have-ya and give me heck
    for the empty bird feeder!
Steller's Jay swagger-nods.
I get up to get the peanuts and seed.
Squirrel moma carries baby balls of fur
    in her mouth, moving them to safety from
      her under-trailer-nest
What? I see you, hopping on my deck chair chattin'-
    away, peering in my window.
I muse, I didn't know I was that trainable.
Thinkin', more thinkin', there are some positive
    things we humans do for
    our feathered and four legged friends.
Coyotes, gather after sunset, at the end of the street.
    They plan, accept their assignments, and implement,
    flawlessly. Some run the flank, into backyards, and flush
    the cats into the marching centre-line canine gauntlet.
Raccoons, water-tap turning taunters
    washing up for dinner
    know their suppliers' household routine.
Steller's Jays, Ravens, and fellow *corvidaes* spp.,
    classical conditioning connoisseurs, conversing and
    crowing over Ivan Pavlov, toying with
    human Injun-newity.
Bears in the peach trees.
Bluebirds atop fence posts.
Raptors on power lines.
Hummers on their feeder's perch.
Hmmm, now I am wondering, like a cat in the bushes
    looking at their "owner", *who is training whom?*

Cartwheel

An Elder told me he'd *seen* a rattlesnake
cartwheel down a hill
SHOT at him like an arrow
tried to bite him
 around the knee.
This happened near a mountain
whose name   sounded
like a bull
when the wind blows through its caves.

Winter

Iced eyelids seeing
sideways slithering snow-snakes
circumnavigating
stormbound snowfield sleds

Flecks of frozen flying light
White out the snowy night

Vonnegut's Medusa

Medusa turned suitors into stone
Water turned armies into sitting mud-ducks

Bernini's last laugh, sculpting Medusa into stone
Vonnegut's Medusa stacked and locked into ice

Carvaggio used Medusa as a shield
Romans trapped her in a Sunken Palace[11]

Turner's Regulus eyes, lids sewn open wield
A Roman General's captured vision, remains silent

---

[11] Basilica Cistern, Istanbul

Praiano, Italia

White emotion limestone seams
Turquoise tangled Amalfi coast dreams
Blue fish and Sirens play
Lemons yellow, basilico scents the day
Green seeping vertical gardens please
Emeraldo breaths of Tyrrhenian seas

Tutto Per Tutti, a palate's emporium
Everything for Everyone tucked among inns
Paulo Sandulli sculpts hour upon hour
Within his hallow-Romanasque tower
Chalk-clay busts of local grizzled fishermen
and pink mermaids flirting with denizens

*Experience the ancestral need to loose
oneself within nature's infinite realm.*[12]

Unknown poet in Praiano, Italia, author's photo of a tile-poem on a house

---

[12] Praiano Tourist Guide, 2008

Pompeii's Roman Codes

I had a dream
that the Romans used
multi-coloured marble tiles
to encode messages on floors and walls.
I wonder what secrets underlay?
The closer to Caesar the greater the fear.

Syrenuse

On Syrene's lap
     lay splayed a smoky body
     her son Tyrrhenian sea.
Her Mary's tears
     splash his smoggy sphere.
In Vesuvius' heat
     water dissolved filthy
     back into Syrenuse
     to heal.
Maybe he will arise pure, in a millennium
     at Zamzam, or
     over Bernini's four rivers, or
     as diamond-mood-music-splashes in Nishat, or
     bubbling up the grasslands at Soda Spring, or
     as a Crescent Moon in China's desert, or
     soothing wounds as Ojo Caliente's honey, or
     flowing down Generalife's water staircase, or
     as drips on vines in the Hanging Garden, or
     up sacred roots in San Miguel Tilquiapam?

Lovers' River Gaze

Among sweet sad words
whispering eyes dart among
rocks and syllables

Bouncing Betty

Been bottom bouncing with Bouncing Betty
Not the bomb, the rubber fishing weight
Flossing sockeye
Just snagged her on a river rock
I snapped my line

One Betty, a red number two hook
A three way swivel
Onto my light casting rod
Cast awaaay out into the Thompson River's
        Sockeye Lane
Fish on! Fish On! Wow!
Holy shit the fighting attitude of this fish
        is so inspiring, after all his travels
This guy is so amazing!
I now have felt in my heart, bones and blood:
        Sockeye attitude
As they traveled the full moon path
I am sure there is not one complaint
        or, whining excuse amongst the bunch
I will never forget how
        I got schooled by that male sockeye.
I only took one
        on the evening of September 23, 2010
We ate the whole fish, filet for supper
        Hugulzum fish soup made with **ALL** the rest
Nothing wasted,
        in honour of my sage friend[13]

---

[13] The best way to ruin a good hunting trip is to kill something (my son's favourite saying). Trucks and bucks, deers and beers, is the way out here in Prince George. My boys went hunting near PG, and we did not get anything but did see a bear marking tree with a very tall and big grizzly mark.

The Vacuum

This is my rant.

If human ingenuity seeks out humility, it may look no further than the vacuum cleaner. The vacuum is a testament to human's enduring gullibility and tolerance for the inane. Archaeologists and anthropologists will look back upon our wireless days, and wonder: "What the hell were they thinking?" My vacuuming mantra, as I haul, lug, untwist, bump, pull, push, pack, wrestle, stretch-reach, yank, kick, unplug, plug back in, wheeze, cough, curse, and yank some more, is: "This albatrossian-boat-anchor SUCKS!" For a hundred years the thoughtful, helpful, ergonomic, economic, technologic re-design of this chain-gang-shackle lay await in a technological vacuum. Oh, we can surely chat on iPads or have robots build cars, but yet to be built, is a vacuum that soothes the nerves, and ultimately does its intended job - sucking up dirt, as opposed to spreading, reshuffling, blowing, stirring, and whipping up allergen storms. I am sure the highlight of the day for our pets is watching the vaudevillian headliner: **Red Skelton vacuuming**. Mark my words, a major milestone in human history will be the invention of a quiet and user-friendly vacuum. Sound science produced the vacuum cleaner. Now your guts should stir, and worry bells ring, when you hear a politician proudly hail "Our environmental policy is based on sound science!" Now you know they are just sucking and blowing at the same time.

Levator labi superioris alaeque nasi

Teasing American Friends

Americans put their winch
>on the rear of their 4x4s

Canadians put their winch
>on the front of their 4x4s

Americans back out of a mud hole
>and go home

Canadians keep on
>a-rockin' eh!

Nigots[14]

Alone, I traveled and recalled
       how they had died right here
I shifted on the hill, down to third gear
This car lurched and chugged as if it was full of fear
Tow truck driver said: "worst crash of my career"

Their van lost its brakes, six cousins died right here
Kept up their roadside memorial every year
It happened so fast, their souls trapped right here
So sudden, too sudden,
       for their spirits to comprehend the end
They didn't know what happened
My old car gasped, slowed and misfired
As I passed the plastic roadside flowers
Alone, I could hear a whisper:
       "please wait for me right here"
The air was electric and my hair stood straight up
Pressing the accelerator, my car the same thought
We passed, whew I am in the clear
I took a deep breath, to clear the fear
I glanced to my right
       my dead cousin
       was effortlessly
       floating over the back seat
       to sit by me.
Desperately she asked *"cousin, did I die right here?"*

---

[14] Gitxsan word for ghost.

Awakening

Every day
Every morning
A cool splash of fresh water
Trickles down her cheeks, tinkles
Down her neck flattens wrinkles
Her sunrise discipline seeks frigid clarity
Moments on skin, a din freshness-glow
Turgid primal jolt ignites taught folds
Grasp and clasp of clear-cold
Corporal sensation flows
Rejuvenates
Beauty

Every day
Every morning
Going to the water ritual
Puts fire in her warrior eyes
Breaths from the ancestors'
Visceral conversation with water
Awakening purity of the
Luminous swan
Fountain of
Youth

Every day
Every morning
Indigenous bathing presents
Freshness of true beauty to others

Inspired by Gaston Bachelard's writing in *Water and Dreams* as well as First
Nations going to the water ritual.

The Future

Humans are over confident in their ability to predict the future. The future is not ours to know. You can make a life plan, but life won't listen. The future has questions.

Nimbleness is friends with hope, faith and gratitude. There is serenity in knowing you are terrible at predicting the future.

We live in a state of constant anticipation.

A painting may fall from the wall.

Photograph by author, a Vancouver street sidewalk note.

Corvid vs. Covid

Wind brings an unannounced visitor

It's breath icy, bony and greedy
Mathematically killing so speedy
Cough into your sneeze
In flew Enza on a breeze

Toilet paper prophets' spiel
This shit just got real!
Shelter in place
No hands to your face

Superheroes beckoned at seven
Hail Grandmother Raven
Help! We're a handshake away from death
She paints each Covid virus red with her breath[2]

---

[2] My Grandmother was a Gitxsan healer (halayt) that worked side-by-side with Doctor Wrinch, in Hazelton, BC. Indigenous knowledge and Western Science can be woven together. This poem and my artwork are meant to be a tribute to health care superheroes.

About Author

Michael Blackstock (Ama Goodim Gyet), Independent Scholar

Michael is a visual artist, poet, professional forester and chartered mediator who lives in Kamloops, British Columbia, Canada. He is of European and Gitxsan First Nation descent, belonging to the House of Geel, Killer Whale clan. Michael's research focuses on Indigenous traditional ecology and trust-based mediation. Michael has a Bachelor of Science degree in Forestry (University of British Columbia) and a Master of Arts degree in First Nations Studies (University of Northern British Columbia). Michael writes fiction and non-fiction works and typically creates visual art works which further comment on topics such as water and indigenous justice. Michael has written two books: *Faces in the Forest: First Nations art created on living trees* (McGill-Queens Univ. press, 2001) and *Salmon Run: A florilegium of aboriginal ecological poetry* (Wyget Books, 2005). Michael is a member of UNESCO-IHP's expert advisory team on Water and Cultural Diversity.

Poetics
"I am just in poetry for the money," announces Wyget, the raven. My poetry is water and water is my poetry. And in the words of the modern-day cowboy poet, Mike Puhallo: "I don't let the truth get in the way of a good story-- but I still try and make it real." As a poet I am at-the-ready to run the ragged edge; when my plan hits black ice, I will engage the hubs into four-wheel drive. Ingredients for my poems: elbow sweat and blessed visitations from characters of everyday life walking through my door, or on the breath of my ancestors. Poetry is a reservoir for culture and identity. One day you will understand what I am doing.

Contact Information:
e-mail: blueecology.mb@gmail.com

Manufactured by Amazon.ca
Bolton, ON

20995050R00049